SPIT

TEETH

Ashlee Karlar
Alison Paradoxx
Chiara Gabrielli
Nico

PAROXYSM PRESS

Paroxysm Press
PO Box 3107
Rundle Mall
Adelaide
5000
[Australia]

www.paroxysmpress.com
www.facebook.com/paroxysmpress
www.twitter.com/paroxysmpress
www.instagram.com/paroxysmpress
paroxysm@paroxysmpress.com

DISCOUNTED
Ashlee Karlar, Alison Paradoxx, Chiara Gabrielli, Nico
ISBN 978-1-876502-24-9

Cover art: **Meg Wright (Red Wallflower Photography)**

Ashlee Karlar

Dad

"Death is never pretty" the nurse said

"We arrive kicking and screaming and sometimes we
leave the same way"

Even after you flatlined you squeezed my wrist

Neither dead nor alive

Still salt
and water
and grunt

Refusing to let go

Perhaps we were more alike than I realised.

Nectarine

My co-worker asks me to describe my boyfriend and I
answer in safe pronouns *they, they're, them.*

"but you're too pretty to be gay" & my mouth o p e n s like
a wound.

I hold her hand on the train and a man calls me a
"worthless dyke" my sexuality leashes me to his voice
box, and he can drag me where ever he wants to.

The taxi driver refers to my girlfriend as "sir" and I ask
him how his day was. She tells me I am enabling
ignorance, but I tell her I am surviving.

My dad "doesn't care" that I am gay but tells his friends
my boyfriend couldn't come to the party.
I smile and change the subject.

It feels like eating a
summer nectarine and swallowing the stone.

Ode to my stretch marks

My stretch marks refuse to hide
behind coco butter or fishnet.

They vivaciously snap gum as they sun themselves
Pink string bikini fragile
Open mouthed and burping on a beach towel.

On weekends they parade the streets in combat boots and eyeliner;
all tantrum and stomp and yell
refusing to apologise for bitch face
spitting at the feet of men who tell me how to smile.

On my lower back a nursing home of 11 silver
grandmothers quietly play cards and share stories about
the old days
They like to slow dance, smoke cigarettes and shimmer.

My stretch marks make a mattress out of my inner thighs
they reach with red fingers
as they scramble for more space
Loud, raucous, greedy,
they trumpet their proud vicious feminine

they shout the woman inside of me is bursting at the seams.

Smoulder

When I was 13
I was told that if a boy ever touched me
to call "fire" instead of "rape"

that bystanders would find the idea of flames more
alarming than the sexual violation of my body
Maybe I can be the fire and the burning house at the
same time

Maybe I am both the kohl and the hooded eyelid
Maybe I was a match before I ever was a girl

Things I am when I am not being a feminist.

I am a riverboat full of red wine. You must bail out buckets of liquor to get into me. I am a haggard split fingernail, embarrassingly unfeminine, free of sparkly nail polish but still parading. I am garish in a startled way- like a mouth full of teeth with a cold sore. I wear glasses while sipping hot tea, steamy and fish eyed. I remember to write poems everyone can relate to, especially old white males. I walk past men on the street and try not to listen to whether their footsteps slow down behind my back. I am often grabbed in bars and am told to "calm down" when I howl at them, face full of righteousness, fists full of girl. I am a hurricane of female emotion, too much for the boys club, all cry or fuck or crying when I should be learning how to fuck, how I should keep it to myself, be pleasant, be 'given one.' This body is reduced to a faucet of sweat or tears and it cannot do more than run. I let my boyfriend put his hand over mine and he marvels at the size difference. He tells how easily he could break me. I know he's saying it to make me feel safe, but all I hear is "you're lucky I haven't had to."

Ode To The Pussy

STRAIGHT GIRL prefers pretty names for her vagina-
'flower',
'yoni'
she wraps it up in black lace and
vedazzles it.
meditates while sitting on a jade egg,
uses organic tampons and sometimes a moon cup,
does kegals on the treadmill at the gym.

STRAIGHT GIRL learns to tuck herself away deep inside her underwear,
uses femfresh like clockwork
Wears activewear on the street to hide her transparent
gets catcalled anyway;
The swing of her hips is an invitation
that she wishes she could shove into the bottom of her gymbag
like a mobile phone;
or a parking ticket.

STRAIGHT GIRL'S boyfriend demands she shave away her overgrown.
Wants more woman/ less jungle,
said the untamed parts of her do not sit well in his stomach
that his spoon-fed diet of dirty magazines left him too soft to navigate
her thicket.

STRAIGHT GIRL warns me that she does not look like the girls in those
pictures.

She draws chalk outlines
around the parts of herself she wants to cut off.
Makes a murder scene out of overflowing edges;
Folds herself smaller just like you asked her to
Spread thighs to get a little kindness
woman
Another nasty girl needing to be cut

That's just like a female, isn't it?

I tell STRAIGHT GIRL
that she
is the proud owner of a beautiful pussy.
That I dream about
blowing cigarette smoke inside of her as I lounge between her legs

that in the morning when
she smells like unwashed clothes,
and honey

I will worship at the altar
of her ingrown hairs
stretch out her lips with my teeth
and bite.

Postcode Wardrobe

I dress myself up for him.

Coat my lashes long with finished high school.
Blush my cheeks with university degree.
Buckle myself into an 'I worked 45 hours this week' coat.

My loud-mouthed father leans quiet against bleached white hospital sheets,
now a soft-spoken skeleton who vomits up everything he eats-
his stomach is an alley cat so used to being kicked it hisses and spits
even in its sleep.

The smirk eyed doctor ushers me into his office and informs me that
this disease is unshakeable.
I wonder if he means the cancer or the poor?

Those torn-jean extra minutes that follow us into waiting rooms,
unexplainable delays on pain medication because he walked in with
a stained shirt
I mean look at him
obviously, he's just in it for a hi-excuse me were actually still
waiting on a doctor over here?
Thank you.

It is as if they are unable to separate low income from patient,
patient from privilege, privilege from prejudice.

I know this game.

It's when people ask where you're from and you dress yourself up in
the hand me downs of the next suburb over.
When you push your own postcode to the back of your wardrobe
like a undesirable dress code.

When they tell me
that poverty is a virus in my blood,
in this body,
that it will chase me howling through tax brackets
I want to say - no

What you will never understand is that
these calloused hands may shake with the ache in their upbringing
but they have learnt how to make art out of spray paint and smashed
windows.
I dress myself down for him.

Soup splattered forearms, frown lines worn as lipstick.
It's just us, now.

GIRLS NIGHT

So I was thinking that tonight
could be, like, a girls night?

We could talk about yeast infections and drink strawberry margaritas.

Maybe we could paint our nails salmon and watch true crime documentaries-
Feast our mascara'd eyes on that dream boat Ted Bundy

We could listen to the narrative about the young pretty girls that became
his victims

And then
(Unironically)
end the evening by calling our friends to make sure they got safely home.

Maybe we'll take an Instagram photo,
caption it as "me and my bitches"

You know? Just a pack of female dogs

It will be like our first job
where, as we spray and wiped the counter

The pimply supervisor would look up our skirt

On the days we wore pants
he'd spit on the ground and say
"You know, you're a real moody bitch sometimes"
And we would blush and giggle along

because he was the one that was signing our paycheques
And what kind of dog survives when it bites the hand that feeds it?

Let's talk about being afraid of our own bodies
How we still suck our stomaches in when our lover fucks us
Because we remember the boys in blue jeans comparing girls waists
How they held out two dirty palms and cupped them together into
perfect sized belts

Let's talk about how every morning girls wake up
and hold the word "help" between our teeth
then spend the day deciding whether to swallow or yell

Let's talk about feminism- I mean, that's a girls issue, right?

Let's talk about how
even after everything

that has tried to kill us

We are still so beautifully alive.

BACKHAND

That summer that I took my clothes off for money, a girl that I worked with fell in love with me. We would spend hours between clients massaging coconut oil into each other's bodies and browning in the sun. Our skin became bronzed dollar coins; draped like bedsheets over our gaunt ribcages. We went out to dinner and drunk cheap wine, squawking over each others star signs. She taught me how to speak Spanish, how to wear my Levis in the bathtub so they glued themselves to my thighs, how to stick a garlic clove up my pussy if I thought it smelt like fish. We never passed third base because I didn't want a girlfriend who let others see her naked. Hypocrisy thumped through the house like a heartbeat. We all whispered about the girls who were rumoured to do 'extras'; as if there is more honour in only showing your pussy and not letting anyone touch it. A girl that we knew began escorting and got gang raped by six men in a hotel room and she didn't go to the police because they would only tell her that she deserved it. That's when I realised how much danger we were really in; how every pole became a post we could be tied to, how easy a caress can turn into a backhand. When I tell people now about the hours I spent there I make sure I tell them the good things I did with the money. Whoring is only good if you do it for a cause. So how do I say that sometimes I miss it? The thrill of a fist full of fifty dollar notes. The way bodies sometimes smelt like sweet rubbish burning on hot pavement in the sun. How older men struggled to look me in the eye, how they fussed with their stomach, kicked at it like a quilt that had gathered at the bottom of the cover, the way they'd thump and stretch and flatten. How do I say it was the one time that my body stopped being something I was scared of and became something electric, something powerful, naked currency in a busy market place; "What do you want to do? How long for? What's in it for me?"

THE DAY THAT I STOP WRITING POEMS ABOUT MY DEAD FATHER

He wakes up and tells me that I was crazy for spending so much money on his funeral.
Tells me he'd rather dig a hole with one hand blindfolded
don't I know people in this world are starving?
Calls me stupid until I'm pink and flushed and then tells me he loves me without taking a breath.

I call in sick to work for a week and we line up his prescription bottles in the gutter
he pulls his tee shirt up proudly and shows me the jellyfish scars that whip across his abdomen
made of tougher stuff than that!
His stomach is a brown protruding balloon full of hot air
that didn't learn to shrink, or shrivel.

Gone is the raspy hum that falls from his mouth with a voice box destroyed-
instead he bellows across our dead grass that its my turn to take the trash out
don't I think it's fucking time I did something around here for once?
And our neighbours come out onto their porches to watch his vowels clatter and smack

Now every Sunday my father makes spaghetti
mixes in vegemite and peanut butter the way they taught him to in jail
his quick laughter sautés itself in the bottom of his belly, browning up the gullet
as I help blend and beat and thicken.

At my engagement party my father makes a speech about being proud of me.
We dance to a slow song and I am a small child and an adult all at once.

We move him in next door,
throw out his old TV with hard rubbish.
It rusts on the street with other things that didn't work
like chemotherapy, or the bible.

This time,

the cancer is not fatal.

Instead it is a small jellyfish, a white scar,
something he will feel the ache of each September, rub his fingers over
& think "how lucky I am to have survived."

Alison Paradoxx

Selective Mutism

selective mutism
came for her at the age of four,
when their kitchen blazed
flames like warpaint through her hair
she is fight or flight
volcanic dynamite
a raging accident that was never
meant...

to happen

so she begins to swallow her voice into
pretend smiles
her body now a
news headline
screaming emergency evacuation alarms through
her skin she is
the property of everybody else...

but herself

and by age thirteen
she has muffled all her words under
seventeen surgeries

one thousand one hundred and
ninety-five sutures
          line   up   on   her
bookshelves in place of her
childhood fairy tales

her scoliotic spine is a   twisted
                    column
                    of
                                        angry
                                bull
                    ants
aflame with all the sentences
she has
trapped
inside her torso

I guess even silence gets
too heavy to carry
after a while...

but she stays quiet
and at eighteen
invents imaginary flesh on her bones that
only she could see as she
starves out her secrets behind a
neon billboard made of unexpressed scars

she is braille   lost in translation
a rainbow on a   black-and-white TV

and at thirty-seven
the septic run-on sentence of her body is a
broken metronome of
sickness, ticking   wildly   out of   sync   with
the rest of the world and she is
tired
of being
quiet

then this thing called 'poetry' comes along.
It slaps her in the face with it's dancing textures, as she

begins to feel every adjective she ever
clenched into fists come cascading out the
pores of her fingertips

because on this stage,
the beating flames of our stories ignite into

a beautiful cacophony of cracks
and imperfection
words like bullets ricochet from tongues
missiles to ear-drums

we are poetry

and on this stage,
we no longer need to be

quiet

anymore.

My existence should have come with a warning label

my existence should have come with a warning label

I searched e v e r y w h e r e for my warning label, but all I found were
bruises... holding my joints loosely together with
frayed parts of my sadness

and you cried as you patched me back together for the
seventeenth time
that week

and you said...
"your existence should have come with a warning label"

as the determined mayhem I live in becomes a
tangle of chaotic sentences I never

finished, a
shambles of emotions I never

unravelled

my body lingers...
... lost in a flux between pain and numbness

and I climb the walls to get higher
frantically failing to escape
from
myself

my existence should have come with a warning label

and the constant sting of blood tests to my
bruised and swollen limbs become
as gentle as gunfire
in a library
a cricket bat to the
head
a sledgehammer to a
watermelon
a vacuum to a
rainbow.

my existence should have come with a warning label

my youth, now a lost
song lyric, thought of in my sleep yet
never written down

I am
a titanium spine
a lifetime of addiction
an obsessive compulsive jumble of
violently raw nerve-endings

my finances, now lost to an endless supply of
medication bills

as my parents
shake their heads and sigh...

... "your existence should have come with a warning label"

and in this tormented wilderness
my intellect fights for survival

and all my nightmares come to
make perfect sense for

the silence is
deafening but the noise
is serene and

here... well, the drugs are
free but the price you
pay for the stay is
more than you were willing to
let go of and...

though I never usually talk about my
sickness with others

today...

today

I couldn't help but feel
as though

     my existence should have come with a fucking warning label.

Conversations around a dinner table

in this house

we don't ever say the things that should
be said...

... yet we all fight to be heard

in this house

we don't talk about the things
that mean a lot but
we talk a lot about the things
that

don't
mean
a thing

I was your invisible child
the pencil set that never came in
colours

the shadow that could never find
the fucking pavement

the one that carried around
disfigurement on my
face and wore it like a
badge of shame

and you couldn't bear to look at me
for my identity became...

a reflection of your own

pain
in my frail,
crash-test dummy body

but how loud does a person have to shout
to be heard?
I shouted so loud that I wore my scars
on my skin like a
neon billboard

and I kept shouting at you
my anger and aggression culminating in a
grand finale of confronting hip bones
a "fuck you" display made up of
emaciation and bitterness
yet still I felt you never heard me

and so I find
myself still
shouting at you

our conversations around
the dinner table fuse angry
words into sharp compass
points tearing holes into
fragile tissue paper

as the soldering irons of my eyes
singe my eyelashes and
bore holes through my
memories

I am twelve kinds of sick today
and despite what you may say ... ten of them are *not*
my own fault

my body,
now an
accidental time-bomb of
disasters

I'm a strange walking paradox of
contradictions
and addictions
that even I... don't understand

and so

I just
keep
shouting

because

in this house...
we don't ever say the things that should
be said...

... yet we all fight
to be heard

Floral Peroxide

tiptoeing on eggshells
with sledgehammers for shoes
she's a vacuumed up rainbow

floral peroxide

hurls molotov cocktails through
her own windows just to run
from herself / bottles tears in porcelain

floral peroxide

she is arrhythmic pulses / site specific electrodes
the colour-coded lead wire on an
ECG machine

she is never / 100% accurate

distilling jars of yesterday
on the shelves of her tomorrows
she is breaking eye contact
with broken dreams

floral peroxide

paints her curtains black / to
trap the sunlight in
sucks on lemon rind / forgets
to drink the gin
she's a crumpled paper sick-bag on a
jet plane to the stars / riding without brakes and a
helmet made of glass
a shiny paper windmill at a circus
with no children

floral peroxide

she is the warp in the record
kaleidoscopic styrofoam
every drop of saline in an
intravenous cannula

throwing pieces of herself
into a magnetised tourbillon
filled with missing postcard memories

floral peroxide

splinters fragments off her wings
with her dehydrated veins
fragile violent glacial
cerebral hurricane

she's a diagnostic flowchart
she's both the smoking gun / and witness
gentle babies jugular
passive motion sickness
she's ...

floral peroxide

Leaving my body

The day I left my body I was four years old.

I wore red dungarees.
I remember how the paramedics
had to cut those dungarees
from my burning body
with scissors...

...because they were my favourite
dungarees.

I remember the screaming

I'm not sure if it was my
voice but my mouth

was moving.

I become used to the sad smiles of the cleaners
in my disinfected hospital cell...

and I always
smile back as the smell of
Dettol
and bleach
and rubber gloves
burn my nostrils.

and I learn to stop
eating
because leaving my body
meant leaving behind
all those hands
clamouring at me

all the pain
all the grotesque scars
all the pretending

to be fine

and I master the technique of
guarding my secrets
behind an iron-clad shield
made from silence
and pretend smiles
and it feels wrong to still
seek sick comfort in
the familiar scent of
antiseptic swabs...
... the bleeps of
dialysis machines
lulling me to
sleep like some kind of...
... dysfunctional
fairy godmother

but see, here
without my body
I am uncontaminated
I am clean

I am numb

here I can keep you at a twelve metre
distance from my secrets at all times
while I drown in a sea of my
own torment
and fill my day with obsessive rituals
and I am watching myself in a
foreign film... but no

matter how
hard I try ... I can't switch the subtitles on

I'm high as a kite, soaring above you in
my haze of
malnutritioned delirium
I am on a never-ending ferris wheel of death
and the conductor
won't
let
me
off...

but here I am numb

here I am...
... *superhuman*

the day I left my body I was four years old

but I will
never
stop
searching for it

Kleptomania / Stolen goods - excerpt I

kleptomania : a persistent neurotic impulse to steal especially without economic motive

I used to only take the small things. Just the things that would fit into the back pocket of my handbag; a swift, surreptitious movement of the wrist, as I crouched toward the bottom shelf of the supermarket fridges, pretending to inspect a product down below. I was fast, and I got faster, more brazen.

The small things became larger things, the handbag now full, became a saddle-bag. I would purchase my handbags based purely around their ability to hold contraband in secret pockets. Utilitarian bags for kleptomaniacs efficiency.

The small things became larger things, the saddle-bag now full, became a shopping cart; like those tartan canvas trolleys that old people, or market-goers wheel around. But mine was blue, and cheap, shoddy canvas that never kept its balance on unstable castors. And it had pockets. Secret pockets, side panels, fabric folds to hide a multitude of sins. A pick-pocketers sidecar.

The items became more nonsensical as my addiction grew. What may start as a direct repercussion of poverty, of the need to survive, can rapidly develop into erratic compulsion. The contents of my handbags now resembled a psychological game of 'guess the analogy' - a Rorschach butterfly of miscellany better suited to that of an elderly person with dementia : one small packet of parmesan cheese, two yellow fluorescent highlighter markers, one single peach, a glossy greeting card with the words "You are grrrrrrreat" emblazoned across a cartoon tigers' face. Perhaps a reflection of my traumatised mind. The items made no sense at all, but my life made less sense, at this point in time.

I suppose you do tend to underestimate your sense of audacity, when in the throes of an addictional episode.

39

I haven't felt the need to steal in years. My desolation no longer needing to be satiated with a never-ending stream of self-hatred. But I will always carry my police record to remind me - that although my existence will no longer be dictated by circumstance, my past actions will forever linger.

Like a criminal record. Like stolen goods.

Chiara Gabrielli

Dear reader,
Skimmer,
Finger licker,
Page flicker,

Before you peep and peruse,
I ask you one thing

For me, these words, when typed and printed are flat and too smooth.
They belong with your lips, your teeth and tongue.
Roll them around and savour each one.
Take big bites, or nibble at edges
Taste the hard hitting T's, and those delicious S's,
Above all, please, feel those vibrations in your throat
I hope they reach your bones and the tricky corners of your mind.
It is those small powerful ribbons of sounds shaking through the air
that dictates history, that
start and end wars, that express love, that can cut or can heal.
Do not underestimate them.
They are the true poetry, the rest, just ink.

Pantihosed Soldiers

This is a robbery
    a thievery
    unapologetically
        taking back all that was drained from my veins.
Shaved off my soul. Sneaked and plucked, but sometimes smacked,
like that rip of wax off of skin.
This is a judgement day call.
And I am coming
        for
           you.

Wog boys / Fuck boys / Mummys' boys.

Ohh my goddddd.
You thought you could just spread all over the delicate concoction of
old and new,
        You, ma tu?
          with your overcompensating-ly masculine,
thick necked,
chin first,
chicken dancing personification of a groined thrust. Ma-oh!
You no longer are the poster child of what it means to be birthed by
olive skin queens.

Knock knock   This is a street fight.

So you better call your boys.
All the   Anthonys,
        Antonys,
        Tonys,
        Tones and Dions you've got
because, baby, the wog girls are here. Chick-chick boom!

And our bodies may have been nipped at the ankles,
                                        waist
                                        and neck,
ma dovrete avere paura, perche le nostre nonne e le mumme have
fed us

Fed us more carbs than you can handle, swam in rivers of sauce that
would
                                        make
                                        you
                                        choke.

We shake, demanding space, hips tits and cheeks, Sophia Loren
style "everything you see, I owe to spaghetti" and the hands of the
goddesses before.

This is a Family war, of operatic proportions.

We are armed with our coffee ground vodka smooth voices.
Proof of the passion, vitality and anger we held in our throats, just
for your egos.
Dial up, full volume.
Blast and strip you,
                strip you of the holy female forms you have tattooed
across your dignity
                like a bandaid.
La Madonna can not save you, that bella does not give un catzo
about your fuck boy problems.

Attenzione, pay attention, il bambino.
This is a debt collection.
Grab your bum bag and and start filling.

Start with all the time that you greedily drank out of your own
mothers eyes.
Or with the space you invaded and humiliated,
compressing your girl until she was subserviently thin. Big man next
to small girl.

Next
      stuff all of the confidence you poisoned with fear
as you vomit lazy cat calls from your commodores, techno music
cover up cloned personalities, as Cigarettes drift out the windows.

This is a toast.
To the pantihosed soldiers
that had to sign their life away and sail away to a stolen sandpaper land.

Husband and wife their only ticket for a new life
to give birth to sons who stomped on their daughters.

This is for the daughters
      and the daughters of daughters

The time of the wog boy is dead.
Delete your account
take your three stripe uniform and throw
                    it
                     out.
Because bello, watch as those stripes get dizzy running up and down
up my curves.

Our tongues are thicker our lips are faster.
We are life bringers in earth
          in womb
          in kitchen
Hands up and freeze!

It was us who brought you into this world
              and it is us who are taking
                    you
                    out.

Man Down, Girl Up

Don't be such a girl,
                    he said.
Don't cry,   he said.
Man up, you bitch,
              you pussy,
                    you fag, you girl.
Don't be such a girl, he said.
But I'm a girl - urm *woman*, half the world cried.

We survive 5 days of constant bleeding.
We can bring the life, if
                    we want.
                    Girls just want to have fun!

                         ...Oh and untaxed tampons.

                         ...And easier access to birth
                         control,

                         ...And to not be told to hate
                         our bodies.

And to not,
              Like,
              be,
              Like
              sexually like assaulted, you know?

And I would understand if it was these constricting terms and conditions
of being my gender that
would make you bark,
              don't be such a girl.
              don't be such a girl.
              don't be such a girl.

But its not is it, is it?

Girls are silly.
Girls cry.
Girls are illogical/irrational/menstrual,

and have a fluorescent rainbow of emotions that they let people see
... **yuuuuuuk**.

But let's forget about the battle of the sexes, the venus vs mars,
adam and eve spat we've been
fighting.
You might not want to hear this boys,

but you are dying.

76% of all "successful" Australian Suicides are committed by males.
That might not be poetic, but that's how the shit sails.
This is a man's world, except like,
emotionally,
And that's why i think you are dying to leave it,
like literally.
The answer to this is not being a man,
It's looking at the girls, and do what they can.
While your adam apples grew to choke the emotions in your throat,
Girls practised articulating their pains by wrote.
Each brick of muscle you add to your prize defensive wall,
We learn to reach out when we, or others, fall.

The antidote to this poison has been there since the time,
Someone drew a line, between the social genders of yours and mine.

And yes this is a simplification, overgeneralization of a disease that
is shaping our nation.
Toxic masculinity, fuelled by racial identities and complex sexualities.

but don't use girl as a spit, as a slur,
listen to my plea and you can conquer -

Don't be such a girl, he said.
Well,
Better to be a girl, I said,

than dead.

You, My Tea

You feel delicious, you say.

Your hand gently squeezes my waist.
The dip that slides down from my chest and then up to my hips.
This seems to be a ride you come back to again and again.
You feel delicious, you say. And I just melt.

Sticky drips down fingers, warm tea pooling in cupped hands.
All muscular tension and strength dissolved away for a second. Then
all the impulses of kissing you, touching you, smelling you, ignite.
They are often all simultaneous and overwhelming, but I force myself
to take my time.
I don't want to miss any part of you.

Name

Take time to learn someone's name
                    my Bubbò would direct me.
Practise until your mouth can accurately produce their identity.
It is important
                    take the time.

Your name is a gift given by your past, wear it like a badge because
it is the oldest thing you own.
And no matter where you go
                    or who you become
                    it is always your answer to directions home.

When someone mumbles, stumbles and guesses, do not turn away
                    Do not settle or resign,
                    stare and repeat.

Chiara. 'C H'.

Just stare and repeat.

My grandparental roots cut deep through this world and are filled
with a sacrifice that has

wrapped countless gifts that I am now blessed to possess.

Recipes that I will forever fuck up.

Thin straight hair on my head,
and thick unruly rebels from the eyebrows down.

My loud, fast talking husky voice, and the knowledge that I do not
need to slow down,
But your hearing needs to hurry the fuck up.

And a name that requires a pause and a rethink.

Ch-iara
Yeah that's it

Just like
Ch-amomile
Ch-iropractor
Ch-emisty
Ch-eorgraphy
And jesus fucking ch-rist.

It's not the letters that confuse you but the uncomfortable feeling in your mouth
It's okay, swallow, I'll wait.

You see my name is not just three syllables, consonants and vowels.

It is the wings that brought me here, the story of a matched made who agreed to marry each
other from only a few letters and a photo and with two separate hemispherical promises came
together to make their own new globe.

It is my the story of a poor girl who timed her river washing chores to a line with the break of the
field working even poorer boy.
Making glistening eyes at each other as the river bubbles between them. So he begs for her
hand, and takes her sailing to what they hoped would be their promise land.

A name is so much bigger than the vibrations you produce and
shape.
It is an earthquake,
through blood and bone,
       through love and loss,
              through time and space.

And with that this world grows larger with every new introductory
handshake.
Assimilate is not the goal you should take

So when they mumble, stumble and guess, do not turn away.
Do not settle or resign.
Stare and repeat.
Just stare and repeat,
       stare and repeat,
              stare and repeat.

Swallow,
    I'll wait.

Boy

Boy,
> I have spent too much money on contraception to now be acting like your mother.

Boy,
> I have been waiting too long to claim my womanhood just for you to pout and call me
>> your baby, a baby, baby.

Boy,
> I have consumed and concocked too many ideas for you to build embarrassed,
>> apologetic walls around my beliefs.

Boy,
> I have inhaled too much of your support like growing fertilizer, before I learnt it was
>> all
>>> just
>>>> shit.

Boy,
I have too many moves to be held still like a warm limbed flesh light.

Boy, I have too much HECS debt to be silenced and dumbed just for your comfort.

Boy,
> I work too hard,
> at too many jobs,
> for too many hours,
> to be acting like your dad handing out allowance.

Boy,
      I spend too much on hand cream to constantly have to keep stroking

                           ....your ego.

B-b-boy,
      my clit is too powerful for you to pretend it doesn't exist. I know you are secretly scared of it.

Ooooohh Boy,
      I have sent my body too many love notes to have you claim my beauty as your achievement.

Boy, I have fought too hard for my sanity for you to dump me your emotions to walk you through,   again and again.

Boy,
      I have screamed into my pillow too many times to now be quiet.

Girl, you never thought you would be this girl.
The 'but I love him' girl,
'He will get better' girl,
'You don't know him like I know him' girl,
'He just needs time' -

Girl.
Breathe.

You are no longer this girl,
but he will always, be that boy.

Ode

Ode to the hair of the pit - The armpit.

The stink and sweat strands smooshed against my side boob.
You are a trend, a political statement, a disgrace, a taboo.

Cuticles cornered, boxed and cubed by silly boys and silly girls.
Silly boys and silly girls.

For years you were plucked,
            Shaved,
            Cut,
            Ripped,
            Chemically burnt,
Into faux non-existence.

If I move fast enough, pay more money enough, sit through more
pain enough,
You
Will
Not
Be.

But you just grew, and grew, growing long and thick.

You are black matter drawing in strangers' stares.
Scaring away small minded suitors who thought my fake lashes and
lipstick meant I wasn't
feminist as fuck.

Silly boys silly girls.

But my dear hair pit, it is not you - it is me.
Well actually, it is them.

The "thick eyebrows - you're a freak/

Thick eyebrows on fleek"
Those who can't make up their minds of what beauty is,
What strength is,
What a body is.

So you do you, hair pit.
Grow defiantly and beautifully - a forest outside of gender control.
Deforestionation of feminine bodies into extinction stops with you.

When my arms rise mid-dance - you'll be there.
When my arms rise in defiance - you'll be there.

When they stare
When they celebrate
When they say "it's only cute when blonde skinny
white girls do it"
You   will   be   there.

You are a reminder that I am woman.
I am human.
I am beast.
And beasts do not tame their hair.

Release on Impact

Now, it's that scene,
Teen movie, pop sound track,
Music blaring, no space to spare and
two characters crash,

Ding.
Release on impact

Camera pans to protagonist,
I'm a mess,
Twisting in stress

This is something I've suppressed,
But you've undressed it

You're a light bulb,

Girl warm up and movements slow
This isn't how this normally goes

Glitter, beer and sweat, that's how we met
Crowded dance floor,
haven't seen you move like that before

Breath out in, breath out in,
Breath out in, breath out in,

Double take,
Now I'm just staring,
Eyes flicker
back and daring
Damnnn now you're staring
music's still blaring

Song change, you go to sit and sip
Life's been leading up to this
Blood pulsing in my head
Silence surrounding me instead
And it's that scene,
Feeling fucking fifteen,

Docs tiptoe to your corner,
and I sit, hip by hip
Fingers numb, sounding da-dumb
Stuttering compliments
Your cue, cut to
wait with drunken breathe
Swallow, reset,
It can't be over just yet-
                        And it's our scene,

Lightbulb crush,-crashing through my eyes wide shut
You smile, jaw twitch
Your laugh trickles down my neck,
The phonics vibrate through my chest plate
Nearly winded me, but I retaliate
You move, I move
You move, I move

The camera gets in real tight
Lash freckles.....hair standing up right
The music swells, the people slow
Just you me, tugging on our clothes
Inch-ing - eyes locked in set,
Lips quivering with each breath
Breathe out in Breathe out in

My hidden corners
         you've illuminated
Your curves, flipped me un-orientated
And I'm so sorry if this is unreciprocated but I want to taste you 'til
inebriated
Why I feel for you I can't articulate it
This is anything but uncomplicated
But somehow I feel authenticated
you're a light bulb and im liberated

And ding
Crash Our lips,
         hands
            and hips

Release on impact

Nico

working weakened

People are uniform
in their yawning, empty faces, in their demands and expectations, I'm
out of smiles but still I fake it
I make the same drink 300 times, "Is this one mine?" Dunno, man.
Take it.
Before I know it, my day's been wasted, basically
just waiting out the payslip – I'm near the end of shift-ing feet, left,
right
Alright, clock, tell me how long is left, it says, "eleven more dollars
and 75 cents."
but I'm fuckin' spent.
So I hide out in the staffroom (coincidentally the bathroom) and I piss
away $1.95, and then I guess I
weigh it against my rent
Pick up my pants and wipe all benches down, then twice again, but
for pretend –
it's all for show, y'know, for the CCTV circus – glowing blinks of
robot eyes, no-one inside, but still I
wave to pass the time -bomb, ticking clicks of tongue and rhyme – I
lose my mind.

Fuck it, mop and bucket soak me up, now squeeeeeze, I wonder what
is left? The broken token
shards of trying hard are falling from my every breath, and some are
landing in my chest, a stab of
never-getting-rest, because

I spend all night unwinding, a beer in bed, a bit of writhing, barely a
blink of blank before the blaring
beep's arriving to say 'no sleep for those still striving to say 'success
was worth the stress; was worth
the compromise and crying' get out of bed, dickhead, it's half-5AM,
you shit-kicking fuck, get up
now, go and do it all again.'

passing by

Those bearded blankets once were men
between the tattered threads and cracked beds of fingernails
are their stories, slipping out through mumbled dreamspeak
they barely sleep, but rather,
stop waking. Always waiting.
mostly breaking down in the quiet hours
before being told to move on,
they move on
and leave another day behind them on the corner,
sore and aching
left there to soak into the pavement
lost, along with
the eye contact that none of us make

where are you from

I'm at the bus stop or bar,

Or on my way to class

Or to the river to just sit

When a crumpled conversation starter (wet with spit) hits me in the back of the head

And it leads to, "but where are you from?"

I try to tell you.

But no, you mean *originally* because 'Adelaide, Australia' isn't an exotic enough answer. *Originally*, because you mean to address the image defined by zygomatic arches - the lines that draw attention to my eyes, and, "they're a bit different, aren't they?"

What you mean to say is, "Yeeeh, nahhh nah, but yew ain't woiiyte, aye"

Well, *originally*... maybe I was a haploid deployed from my father, as precedent to target (on accident) the totem ovum. Then a diploid zygote that split itself repeatedly. Eukaryotic keynotes and the luck of Ol' Biology gave my parents an anecdote and a baby unintentionally.

Where are YOU from?

But you're back on ethnicity immediately, and though I've said explicitly that I'm Australian, you press again. "Do you speak any other languages? Like, Asian?"

And then you say that my English is pretty good and that you know someone from Taiwan.

My English is phenomenal. But there's nothing in language for the anguish of somehow being sandwiched between the "us"es and "them"s of Aussie idioms, so I'm left languishing under bandages, without much I can say for the suggested 'advantages' that you're offering my way, like:
"You must be good at maths, then"
and if you're feeling chatty, you'll throw in something about fried rice and eating with chopsticks,
"how good is Kung Pao Chicken?" before the kicker

"Is it true that Asian women are simply hornier? You know, genetically."

I am not good at maths… but I SHOULD be, right? Fet-check 1, 2, and countless times more, I have sworn to myself that this isn't truthful. There's other ways to be useful, and so I used to study hard to then be told I'm not smart, I'm just Asian, and that B+ is a shame. Well it hurts just the same when you point to my name as it's next to my grades, as if there's a clear correlation between genetic donation and my own GPA.

Fet-check, 1, 2, and countless times, too, I have been expected to be subservient in the bedroom. I've been rejected for not accepting (nor swallowing) that ejaculate conjecture. Or for not praising their penis as the biggest I've seen, as if it's the dick of my dreams. I'm supposed to be, "Oh! It is elephantine! Ohhhh what a colossal (!) "--
…. fault on my part, sir. Get out.

I suspect their disappointment was deemed greater than mine, since I must get this all the time
And time again, is fet-check, 1, 2, but this one is times two, and it's, "What are you? Why don't you go back to *where you came from*"

(We've all come across those Southern Cross-eyed motherfuckers…)

But I *am* where I'm from, as I'm from the deepest stretches of my

70

own mind, I am. I've lived in
trenches and lateral lines within the spinning and thinning
hippocampus of mine – where I am, is where I kill time.

What do you mean *from*?
I *am* an indication of a happening event. I'm the point in space that
my words represent. I am the friction of abrasive dissent. *I am what
I'm from*, and I give birth all day long to new capacity. I've been
endless since the beginning, that first split of indeterminate growth –
it kept going, I'm still growing, and y'know… I'm from the fucking
future at this rate.

So what about you, mate? Where are YOU from?

tiff

I'm not sure how long
I've been sick
of the damned walls

Pass out, or
find somebody else to
pass the time?

Her hair is short, it's nice
and neither of us like feeling
hungry
but we are, open mouths
and spit
and little care for mess
on the bed it's the best
until
I roll off

she says,
"I think I'm falling in love with you,"
and then she siiiiiiighs
but I don't look at her
I leave

she follows me for a while
until
I change security measures

safe-keeping

myself inside

headphones

I see her crying in the courtyard
her friend beside, glaring
fire
bombs
hatred and
war trenches twisted around
the lips
they mouth,
"Fuck off"
Fair enough

I barely nod
and change direction

babe calls out,
"whyyyyyy,
how could you
do this to me?"

I think,
"but I didn't do anything,"
before I realise
that might be what she meant
as if I could have known
she didn't know what I'd do,
I…
I don't look at her
I leave

metamorphosis

I am
an adrenaline pen drawing new pathways until I can tell the difference
I'm epigenetically altered
I am
Transhuman, and I don't care if I'm passing
Transducing -- I'm memory churning to turn to energy, the whirling
tide. While I'm becoming
self-centralised once more I'm nothing, I'm one, I'm zero and I'm
both because I'm empty as
in (w)hole
But it's not so deep.

Allow the sequence to stay the same 'cause family history shall
remain as it's always been,
but my blood's now re(a)d between the lines, I'm learning how to
change my mind, I'm splitting
cells and growing kind
I'm growing nervous
May these thoughts be non-invasive, a saltatory exploration with my
attendance mandatory,
I'll sign consent to tell the story -- a concession to confessions, may
we wither without our
woes and go grow senescent with intent
Are you nervous?
I am

Re-introducing; re-naming; re-claiming myself
Is only a matter of time; of frame; of mind
Metamorphosis is just a metaphor for this
change

My amygdala left limbic loops too limp and antiquated, so I learned
to limbo. Now I am the
rim, I hold the edge back from itself, yet I am brimming; spilling over

cup capacity. Pick up the
pieces ever-thankful for all that's ample without apathy.
I am enough.
So I sigh and then collapse. I let my diaphragm relax, decidedly.
Inside of me, something
skips to glitch me back on track,
a circuit's circus
Now synthesising my own easing, I hold poise instead of poison. I
spend my silence saving
noise to raise my voice when I have reason to. The same way acceptance
isn't passive, there
is no peace without a riot first; we resist to name our freedom, and our
ideas come when we
need them
to give us purpose

Re-acting; re-adapting; abstracting myself
I'll leave the skin of last season behind
Metamorphosis is just a metaphor for this
Breakdown that I'm having,
Oh *I've had it* and it's wonderful
I'm electric, I'm potential,
I'm in the charge

"This will pass" has never failed me. I move forward faster and more
fervently, these days so
seamlessly and cyclically at a verified velocity. I advance and I expand.
I develop an
understanding within self-discipline, demanding that I persist; that I
exist. Insisting purpose
under pressure, I am sure to make a fist
as I form new pathways

I'm in charge of the circuit's
I'm *in* the charge
So by my will, I charge forward

now on knowing that I will
be the difference
and I will
change my mind

I bury my friend today.

I remember the day I met him. It was warm and I was restless, and I didn't get much sleep because that damned naked man was singing all night again. At least he wasn't jackin' it this time.

I don't know exactly which day it was but it'd been a few since I'd last taken a good shit – I needed some laxatives. I looked down at my stomach, its distended portion pulsating arrhythmically as if my eyes couldn't process the building pressure, I groaned and got up off the floor. I showered myself in baby wipes and unscented moisturiser. It didn't take me long to decide I'd wear the same clothes as yesterday.

The percolator grumbled as it woke but eventually bubbled into a screaming crescendo. Same, man. Same.

I used too much artificial sweetener but it's just enough to get me up to speed -- time to change
tense, and
I never know which cigarette I'm up to. Sometimes I think I just like the act of rolling them, but then I light one up and I know exactly why I still smoke.

Now I've really gotta take a shit, but I need help.
Woolworths is open in 5min. 7min walk. 'Kay.

There's too much grot, grime, and whatever those flakey white-grey patches of missing mirror are for me to see my reflection well, so I just tussle my hair into a general shape. I get the feeling someone else has been using my toothbrush so I throw it out and gargle some vodka instead, and I'm ready to go.

I forget if I'm wearing shoes, so I look down at my feet and I'm still not sure.

Crossing the road is on a bending blind spot for both driver and pedestrian, but I find it easy to cross because I'm more worried about what the trees are saying about me this time. They're always joking – they've known each other for years.

Towards them to say hello, each blade of grass squeals out from both pain and delight beneath my steps. I never get used to the sound.

I move to the gravel path to grind teeth instead and then something in my neck cracks. I never get used to that sound, either.

Even though I know it doesn't live in this area, I'm always on lookout for the BBC – the Big, Black Cockatoo that chases me down sometimes when I'm on a bus or passing Flinders Medical Centre. It has a screech like a thousand sirens getting dragged down chalkboards with a choir of toddlers' tantrums, and its talons are the long, scaly hooks you expect from dragons. Of course, it isn't here.

"Of course it isn't here," a nasal-pitch scratch at the back of my throat, must have come from that wiry bush. It is staring at me.

I try to ignore it and shoulder past with my gaze averted as if I don't care.

I'm busy, going to the shops.

Reckon I teleported to the playground. Gimme a minute.

Since I don't like the tunnel that's coming up, I decide to take the swing. It's a few bursts to build up the momentum but if I do it right, I can clear South Road and land by that shop-front that's up for lease again. I'll get my breath on the stairs there.

Heaving the hot air out of my lungs only to pull it back in before another cough, it takes me too long to notice the old man with wings slouched beside me and I jump a little out of surprise.

His smile is slight, but it's warm, and more in his eyes than his mouth.

"Hello," I say, unsure.

He doesn't speak but nods once, slowly blinking, then raises back those smiling eyes to me. In that moment, we became friends.
Tense paused and flickered on the iridescence of his lengthy wings in the sunlight.

I slithered down the stairs to slouch beside him and we talked for time on end. Well, I talked, mostly. He'd sometimes laugh, or he'd offer short and playful retort to prompt me into saying more. We got comfortable. I nestled into his four arms and he nestled back, into my cheek.
It's only then that I noticed his broken leg – mangled from the second articulation down. I tense. He's rubbing the misshapen flesh on his other, good leg, as if to mindlessly soothe an ache; as if the break could be massaged away.

Without hesitation I scoop up his frail body and declare, "I'm taking you home."

He struggles at first but loses strength or fight within three metres and accepts the free ride, limbs limp and dangling, his head lolling in time with my stride.

"Y'know," he says to me, his eyes closed towards the sky, "Today's been good."

"Oh, yeah?"

"Yeah," he sighs, "Real good."

We're almost home when he wakes up with a jolt of new energy, exploding out of my arms. I'm relieved – he'd been getting heavy this last stretch. His old, bony body is so exuberant now that I can't help but laugh at him, with him, as he's dancing around his own exclamations, we're both so excited!

Seems he lived a whole 'nother life in that nap.

I do that sometimes, too.

He pushes me down by the shoulders to sit, "I have something I need to tell you," and with a swivel, falls to lean next to me.

He's absent-mindedly rubbing one leg against the other again. I try it out, and find it is kinda nice to start a static tsunami, waving hairs into each other when they might otherwise feel alone.
And that's when he begins to tell me.

He tells me of love born, fostered, lost and mourned. He tells me of how old suns would rise, and how they've been falling in temperature. He tells me of infrared vision that sees through space and time, into the past, and that perspective shifts in a pattern similar to a snake's skeleton in motion. He tells me that idioms begin to make more logical sense after they've been translated into a language 3 countries away, at least 3 times, and that the original 'holy trinity' was always supposed to be art, science, and philosophy, but the intent and meaning of this was lost due to incomplete translations across too few continents. He tells me fear is only an emotion that hasn't yet been 'handled', and its intensity is also its begging to be embraced.

"Every image you've ever seen has already been held and been crumpled, then pressed into leaf and thrown to the wind," he tells me, "so don't worry when you feel you're beginning to drift."

One last breath cascades down the word 'd r i f t ' and in that moment I know that he's gone. Maybe into an old sun, maybe into another snake skeleton, I don't know.
But this body, in my lap, is empty.

"What are you doing?"
My mum appears above me, towering and trembling. Her brow seems to follow her lips around,
"Is that... a cricket?"

I'm looking up at her and she seems to be caught, between curiosity and concern.

It's become a pretty standard facial expression by now and I recognise it immediately.

I'm doing something weird, aren't I.

"It's nothing," I reply in a tone so distant the words are barely audible, "Yeah, s'just a cricket."

I clench my fist and think,
Pressed into a leaf and thrown to the wind.

I bury my friend today.

Ashlee Karlar is a spoken word poet, writer and social worker. A former competitor in the Australian poetry slam, a previous poet in residence and a regular feature performer at open mics across Adelaide, Ashlee's poetry is a cocktail of satirical social commentary and self love odes. A tequila enthusiast, she is also known for her borderline obsessive love of cats.

Alison Paradoxx is a Producer, Performance Poet, Event Host, Peace Foundation Award Winner, Disability Advocate, and State Poetry Slam Champion. She has performed everywhere from The Sydney Opera House, to The Crown and Anchor.
Her first solo production, Floral Peroxide, sold out its 2019 Adelaide Fringe season, won an award, and received a grant to show interstate. She is still getting her head around that one. Alison is currently learning to play the musical saw. She also creates electronic sound art with her partner, 5000AD, and twelve of her vertebrae are made of titanium. Her hair is bigger than yours. She loves you for buying this book. Go make friends with her on Instagram @alison.paradoxx, Facebook or Web : www.alisonparadoxx.com

Chiara Gabrielli is a queer artist living and working on Wurundjeri land. She has her fingers in many pies working as an actor, writer, theatre-maker and poet. Her mum is most proud of her work performing in the Ruby Award winning South Australian State Theatre Company's production 'Gorgon', representing South Australia at the Sydney Opera House in the 2017 Australian National Poetry Slam, and being selected as the Adelaide City Library Poet in Residence. To be in the know on all her small gigs that make up an arts career, and also for just some gelati content, follow her on instagram at chiara.witha.ch or on facebook artist page.

Nico is a finger guns poet who kicks arse, self doubts, loves a beer and isn't afraid to tell you when you're acting like an arsehole. Won a shit ton of money in a huge slam but is just too good to be fucked anymore.

Meg Wright (Red Wallflower Photography) has lived in Adelaide since 2012. You can find her in the vicinity of derelict buildings or photographing local bands. She drinks a vast amount of tea and lives with her beloved, mischevious cat Juniper.
Her images speak for themselves.

Lightning Source UK Ltd.
Milton Keynes UK
UKHW011306251119
354202UK00002B/619/P